Working Together for Professionals in Health Care:
Communication Skills for Collaboration and Teamwork

**Wendy Leebov, Ed.D.
Leebov Golde Group**

Working Together for Professionals in Health Care: Communication Skills for Collaboration and Teamwork

Current Version: Copyright 2012; Wendy Leebov

Original Version; Copyright © 1995 by Mosby Great Performance

Reprinted by CreateSpace; 2012

No part of this book may be reproduced or transmitted in any form or by any means, graphic, electronic, or mechanical, including photocopying, recording, taping, or by any information storage or retrieval system, without the written permission of the publisher.

Requests to the Publisher for permission should be addressed to **Wendy Leebov**; 625 Casa Loma Blvd., Unit 1406; Boynton Beach FL 33435
Fax: 215-893-3524
Email: wleebov@quality-patient-experience.com;
Phone: 215-413-1969

Keywords: Patient experience, patient satisfaction, healthcare training, service excellence, service improvement, excellent service, service quality, patient-centered care, HCAHPS, healthcare quality, leadership development, management development

About the Author

Wendy Leebov, Ed.D is a passionate advocate for creating healing environments for patients, families, and the entire healthcare team for over thirty years, Wendy Leebov has helped hospitals and medical practices enhance the patient experience. Wendy is currently President and CEO of the Leebov Golde Group. Previously, she served as Vice President and change coach for the Albert Einstein Healthcare Network in Philadelphia. A communication fanatic, Wendy has written more than ten books for health care, as well as toolkits, guides, instructional manuals, slide shows, and articles. Wendy's most recent books:
- **Wendy Leebov's Essentials for Great Personal Leadership;** AHA Press, 2008
- **Wendy Leebov's Essentials for Great Patient Experiences;** AHA Press, 2008

Wendy received her Bachelor of Arts in Sociology/Anthropology from Oberlin College and her master's and doctorate from the Harvard Graduate School of Education.

All Rights Reserved © 2012 by Wendy Leebov

ABOUT THIS BOOK

This book discusses co-worker relationships: how to keep them good when they are good and how to improve them when they're not. Your contributions to the overall harmony of your workplace and the quality of work life of your team can be as personally gratifying as your professional achievements. By taking an active role in creating a productive working environment, and by understanding and respecting the behavior and motives of your co-workers, you can enhance the quality of your own everyday work experience, while also being a respected contributor to your organization.

Working Together represents several years of research into improving co-worker relationships and creating the kind of teamwork needed in today's demanding and turbulent health care environment.

This book includes exercises and practical suggestions for improving co-worker interactions. The exercises at the end of the book are designed to raise your awareness of other people's roles as well as your own in improving co-worker relationships. You can do some of these exercises on your own, while others require the participation of co-workers in meetings and role-play situations.

OTHER TITLES IN THIS SERIES:
Assertiveness Skills
Customer Service
Resolving Complaints
Telephone Skills

Introduction

Typically, we spend about 40 hours each week at work. For many of us, that's almost half of our waking hours. It certainly helps when we love the work we're doing, but even the most enthusiastic among us can't always count on that.

When the work isn't all we might hope for, it helps a lot when we like the people with whom we work. But, of course, we can't count on that either.

At the very least, even when we wouldn't choose our co-workers to be our best friends, we hope for cooperative, mutually respectful relationships with them. Unfortunately, we can't count on that either, certainly not all of the time. Even in the friendliest work environment, differences are inevitable and problems are bound to arise.

When problems do arise, they can threaten to interfere with the workings of your team and your organization as a whole. People under stress from interpersonal differences slow down, make mistakes, feel irritable, and may consciously or unconsciously do things that affect the efficiency of your team. And because every person in a team is vital, the team's service to its customers is bound to suffer when co-workers aren't getting along.

In health care settings, conflict among co-workers may impede patient care and service to other customers in subtle—and sometimes not-so-subtle—ways. In addition, important projects and processes may be delayed or may suffer in quality. Friction among co-workers can influence everything that results from your team's work as well as the moods and morale felt by everyone who works with you. That's why it's so important to understand co-worker relationships: how people interact in the workplace, how and why differences arise, what to do when they arise, and how you can personally influence the quality of the relationships you have with other employees on the job.

CO-WORKER CONFLICT AFFECTS PATIENTS AND OTHER CUSTOMERS

When co-workers are feuding-even if they try not to disagree openly-patients, their loved ones, and everyone who comes into contact with the workers involved can sense that something is wrong. Inevitably, friction among co-workers impairs the crucial sense of confidence patients and their loved ones must have in their health care providers. Consider the examples below.

Example #1: The Case of Testy Office Staff

Ralph visits one of his HMO's medical practices because he's concerned about a few gastrointestinal symptoms. As he's waiting in the waiting area, he overhears Jeanne, the receptionist, and Melanie, the patient accounts person, squabbling. Apparently, Jeanne is annoyed with Melanie because Jeanne expects Melanie to handle her phone calls during breaks (which according to Melanie, are all-too frequent!). Ralph and the others in the waiting area overhear this squabbling and wonder, "Are these people trying to escape their work? Is this really a team taking care of me? Am I in good hands?"

Example #2: The Case of the Battling Nurses

Anita Came to Memorial Hospital for a surgical procedure to insert a shunt in her chest so that she could receive powerful doses of chemotherapy to treat her Hodgkin's disease. The two nurses preparing her for the surgery were obviously engaged in some kind of dispute. They bickered openly with each other, while Anita, already distressed by the prospect of the surgery, tried to tolerate the tension in the air.

Finally, after some time, she spoke up: "It makes me nervous to have you two at odds with each other while you're taking care of me." The unconvincing response was: "Don't be silly. We're not letting it interfere with the attention we're giving you."

Anita was not at all reassured by their words. She worried about a nursing team that would not or could not set aside personal differences long enough to do its important work. An already distressing situation for Anita was made even worse by the inability of co-workers to get along..

In healthcare settings as you know, employees are not the only people operating under difficult conditions. Patients and their loved ones tend to be under great stress themselves. Their symptoms and illnesses frighten them, and their treatment is often as uncomfortable as it is confusing.

Patients and their friends and families expect health care workers to interact harmoniously and cooperatively. After all, if the people who work in health care can't take care of themselves and each other how can they take care of their patients?

YOU CAN MAKE A DIFFERENCE

When co-worker difficulties arise, as they inevitably do, you need not think of yourself as a victim of circumstances. You can choose to be a driving force in improving co-worker relationships, thereby helping those around you, boosting your team's effectiveness, and preventing needless stress in your own life. When everyone plays a role in keeping the workplace running smoothly and calmly everyone benefits. Also, patients, their loved ones, and other customers of your organization sense the staffs harmony and gain confidence in the people providing health care services.

LEARNING TO GET ALONG IS A LIFELONG PROCESS

The processes by which people learn to get along with each other in social and work groups continue throughout their lives. Social learning began for all of us in early childhood, when we learned to "play nice" with our friends. However, even at a very young age, we sometimes got into fights and came away with hurt feelings. We had to be taught how to share, how to give in sometimes, and how to defend ourselves when necessary. A little later, we learned to get along with other children in school, and that's where we began to learn how to work with other people, even when we sometimes didn't like them.

As we grew older, our relationships grew more complex, and the stakes became higher and more serious. Still, almost no one who works or socializes with other people knows exactly how to handle every situation that comes up. That's what makes getting along with other people a lifelong learning process.

Positive Co-Worker Relationships: 10 Principles

We don't often get to choose our co-workers, and we don't always understand or get along well with every member of our work team. Occasionally we must work with someone whose behavior is so abrasive that we wonder why the organization doesn't discharge the person. In some cases, the person's technical skills may be so good and so valuable that management overlooks interpersonal difficulties. In other cases, however, the employee's behavior may be so disruptive that management chooses to replace the person. Whatever the circumstances are, your task, as a member of your work team, is to do your own work to the best of your ability and to enhance your co-workers' ability to do likewise.

That's where the 10 principles of positive co-worker relationships come in. Some of them may seem quite familiar to you. Others may help you see yourself and others in a different way. In any case, if you embrace these principles and try to reflect them in your day-to-day behavior, you'll find that your interpersonal relationships at work will become more and more positive and gratifying. If others do likewise, your work team can resolve almost any problems that arise. Briefly, the 10 principles are the following:

1. Respect people's differences. If everyone you work with were exactly like you, you'd probably get very bored, very quickly. As you know, not everyone you meet comes from the same cultural, racial, religious or economic background that you did. Not everyone had similar childhood experiences, achieved the same level of education, or had the same values and interests. These differences lead to differences in work style, motivation and interpersonal behavior. The fact is, these differences not only make people interesting, they also lead to creative, multitalented work teams with the capability of better serving customers who also are widely different from one another. It's important to respect the differences as well as the similarities among your co-workers. This is a first step in learning to get along in stressful situations. Treating people with respect is a good idea under any circumstances. But for a health care professional like yourself, treating people who are different from you with respect and dignity is an important part of your job.

2. Think positively! Make your positive, upbeat energy and attitude contagious to everyone in your work group. Be conscious of what you're doing and saying. Be sensitive to the effects your actions have on others. Make yourself a role model for positive thought and action. And make your team a better one because you're on it.

Griping, bad-mouthing and complaining rarely do any good. All they do is drag people down. Make your complaints constructive. When you have a problem with a co-worker, talk to him or her directly instead of talking to others secretly. And when you are frustrated with the job, the environment, the quality of work life, or the organization, bring your concerns to the attention of people who can help you do something about them—your supervisor, constructive-thinking peers or higher-level managers—if that becomes necessary. Griping with people who have no control over the situation is fruitless. Instead of endless griping, take the initiative to make things better or come up with suggestions for making improvements.

3. Acknowledge your co-workers. A smile and a hello go a long way toward making people like you and want to cooperate. Break the ice. Make eye contact. Express a few words of interest in the person. For example, you might say, "How was your weekend?" or "I understand your daughter is getting married soon..." Invite people's opinions, ideas and viewpoints. Ask their advice. Let them know that you are concerned for them as people as well as being interested in how they can help you get your job done.

4. Listen. Pay genuine attention to what people are saying to you. Listen to their words and the feelings being expressed behind those words. When someone complains, speaks up or confronts you, pay attention to what they are saying and don't react defensively.

5. Appreciate others. Don't ever be shy about saying "thank you." Tell people that you appreciate what they've done for you. Put it in writing if you wish. A note of appreciation is a very positive and tangible way of telling someone you're grateful for his or her help.

6. Pitch in and help out. Even if it's not your job, step in and take the pressure off your co-workers with or without being asked. After all, you're all part of the same team. Take a call, carry a box to the mailroom, look up the information needed, offer to help when things are slow for you but a little more hectic for a coworker. When you help each other, the job gets done, and you help your customers. That's why you're here! Remember, cooperation is contagious—when you give it, you get it in return.

7. Live up to your end of the job. Follow through on every task. Meet your deadlines. Keep your promises. Everything you do or don't do ultimately affects your co-workers. It's up to you to earn everyone's trust and confidence. People are depending on you; don't let them down.

8. Respect people's time and priorities. Don't distract your co-workers needlessly. If you must interrupt them, ask whether it's OK to do so. Be considerate of other people's time, and be alert to cues that they're pressed and want to return to their work

9. Admit your mistakes. We all make mistakes sometimes, and as much as you'd like to forget it, you are no exception. Admit openly when you've made a mistake, overlooked or forgotten something, or made an unwise decision, and then apologize. People are much more understanding when you take responsibility for your own actions rather than trying to cover up or make excuses.

10. Invest in other parts of your life. It may seem odd to include this in the principles of positive co-worker relationships, but it is true that the more you invest in other parts of your life, the more at ease and effective you are likely to become at work. Too many people make their work the center of their lives, putting every other interest on the back burner. The result is that whenever anything goes wrong on the job, it becomes magnified out of proportion. A small difference of opinion or disagreement with a co-worker can become the most important thing in your life. However, if you develop other interests, if work isn't all there is in your life, you are more likely to keep things in perspective. Also, you'll have more personal experience to bring to your work and interactions at work, making you more effective.

YOU CAN PUT THE PRINCIPLES TO WORK

As you read through the applications of the 10 principles of positive co-worker relationships, relate them to your own behavior and to those of your co-workers. Perhaps you can identify situations in which these principles worked for the good of the team and other situations that could have gone better if these principles had been applied. The key to these principles is effective communication—spoken and unspoken.

Positive co-worker relationships are critical to the smooth operation of any organization. The way staff members interact can determine the personality of an entire department, unit, office, work group and, ultimately, the entire organization. A harmoniously cooperative staff is an efficient staff. When people work together without friction and treat each other with dignity and respect, they are more likely to extend these courtesies to their customers.

It's up to each staff member to do his or her part to make sure that the work setting is as positive and pleasant as possible and that differences are worked out quickly and effectively. The 10 principles will help you do your part.

Before you read more about the 10 principles, take a few moments to try and see yourself as others see you. Then, keep in mind how you think others see you as you read and apply the 10 principles.

HOW DO YOU THINK OTHERS SEE YOU?
- **If you listened to your co-workers talking about you, what do you think they would say?**
- **How warm and positive would their feelings about you be?**
- **What do you think your co-workers most admire about you?**
- **What fault would they find with your work or your personality?**

Now, let's explore the 10 principles of positive co-worker relationships again, in greater depth. Consider how you can build on your strengths and improve on your weaknesses, so that you will be valued more greatly and perhaps even treated more courteously and respectfully by your co-workers.

PRINCIPLE #1: RESPECT PEOPLE'S DIFFERENCES

Each of us is a unique individual, with individual experiences, interests, expectations, background and abilities. That fact can make things interesting, but often it also makes life difficult.

As a health care worker, you have at least a few things in common with your co-workers. You all work for the same organization and you might all live in the same geographical area. Your interest in health care is a common bond that can bring you to overcome some differences.

But differences in gender, cultural background, race, religion, nation of origin, age and life experience all have the power to drive people apart. Sometimes, people misunderstand other people's language, gestures, intentions and actions because of these differences. They react as though people different from them were somehow strange or inferior. When that happens, feelings of distance, fear and discomfort are triggered. To overcome these feelings, it's important to see differences as positive and interesting, not negative, and to take steps to build bridges of understanding between you and your co-workers, instead of walls of fear and misunderstanding.

You might also differ from certain co-workers in your personal work style. Some people, for example, like to concentrate on one thing at a time, staying with a task until it's finished. Others like to work on several projects at a time, switching from one to another but always managing to finish all of them on time. Some people prefer to work by themselves; others work better when the task calls for working with others. Some people like to get difficult tasks out of the way in the morning, and others are ready to tackle them in the afternoon. You may really enjoy public contact, dealing with patients over the phone, or working with patients in person. Your co-worker may cringe at the thought of having to deal with the public and may prefer to concentrate on doing paperwork or preparing the materials, information, supplies or equipment needed to serve patients and other customers. Because any health care team has many different kinds of work to do, many different kinds of people, with different talents and interests, are needed to perform the team's work and make the team tick.

Sometimes we don't understand why somebody else might not like the things that we like or want the things that we want. You may be very career oriented, hoping to advance to bigger and better things, while your co-worker might be content to stay at the same job even though it's fairly low on the organizational ladder.

Fortunately, you don't need to share another person's motives, needs and preferences to respect them. Although it's nice to make friends, that's not the primary reason most people go to work. Even if you wouldn't necessarily want to socialize after hours with particular co-workers, you do have to work together. You would do well to find the positive aspects in their personalities and appreciate their contributions to the functioning of the organization and to your team. You don't have to agree with people on all levels to work well with them. All you have to do is appreciate their good points and respect them for who they are and what they contribute.

But let's not stop at just tolerating other people's differences. There's a lot to be learned and gained from people who think differently than you do. You could use such differences as the basis of a relationship and learn a lot about yourself in the process.

For example, suppose that you are outgoing and love working with people, but your co-worker seems to be happiest doing lab work alone and you can't understand her preferences at all. Try approaching her and saying something like, "You really do seem to enjoy working alone in the lab. I think I'd find that a bit lonely. Why do you like doing that instead of working with other people?" Don't put your co-worker on the defensive; just ask a question. You may learn a little bit more about her and why she works the way she does. Or suppose that your co-worker is from another culture and does things that mystify or confuse you. Have the courage to express your curiosity and learn from him. Your co-worker's answers to your questions may open lines of communication that otherwise might have remained closed. You may learn something about yourself in the discussion as well. Most important, you will develop a greater appreciation for the fact that it takes many different kinds of people to make up an effective staff.

Teams also gain effectiveness when they include different kinds of people. Different people have different contributions to make, different talents, different capacities, and different preferences. A team that's too homogeneous tends to be ineffective. Imagine the nursing home where everyone was hired because they excel in compassion. If it turns out that none of these people is meticulous about the technical aspects of their jobs, the residents of this nursing home would not receive the quality of medical care that they might need. Their rooms might be dirty and their food cold when it should have been hot. Your team needs diversity in order to be able to effectively do the broad range of things required of it.

BUILDING UNDERSTANDING
Instructions: ONE-on-one with a co-worker, discuss the quality of your work life along the lines listed below.
1. What parts of your job are most satisfying?
2. What pars of your job are least satisfying?
3. What motivates you to do a great job?
4. What do you need/want from the people you work with-what's most important to you in your co-worker relationships?
5. What strengths, abilities, and qualities do you bring to the work team?
6. How can I support you better and help you make your work more productive and satisfying?
7. What are some of your ideas and suggestions for improving our relationship?

PRINCIPLE #2: THINK POSITIVELY!

Working with people who have a positive attitude about themselves and about their work is easier than working with people who tend to be negative. However, it is often very tempting to get along by going along. That is, you might find yourself engaging in negative behavior because that's what everyone else is doing or is in the habit of doing.

Most of us have been in work situations where friction and disagreements made work difficult and unpleasant. Bickering and complaining drag everyone down and solve nothing. Some people seem to thrive on bickering among themselves, complaining about everything, and bad-mouthing other people. Perhaps such behavior keeps their lives interesting, or perhaps they feel frustrated and powerless in the face of conditions or people they wish were different.

Co-workers who constantly complain are draining to be around. Though some people may sympathize with their co-workers' frustrations and perceptions, they don't see the point of joining in with negativity, bad-mouthing others or the organization. When some people on a work team dwell on the negatives and others do not, the conflict can be very disruptive. The people who don't join in may want to appear sensitive and understanding, and therefore find the constant naysayers hard to deal with. As a result, they listen to endless complaining because they are unable to cut it short without appearing impatient, insensitive or superior.

To deal with habitual complainers, start by watching your own behavior and making sure you're not one of them. And when a co-worker who is a broken record of gripes and frustrations does frustrate you, have the courage to do something about it. Otherwise, you're letting yourself become the victim. Speak up and say something like, "Art, every day at lunch you complain about something that drags you down. Frankly, I get tired of listening. I find it affects my energy for work. Can we talk about something else?"

Of course, nearly everyone can find something to complain about from time to time. The positive way to handle problems is to identify them in a concrete way. Get specific; pinpoint what's bothering you and your co-workers, and think or talk through possible solutions. It's quite possible that some things can't be corrected. That's inevitable. The people with a positive outlook and good coping skills manage to let go of these frustrations and accept the situations and conditions they know they cannot change. Instead, they concentrate energy and attention on those things that can be corrected and resolve to do something about them, or bring them to the attention of someone else in the organization who can help if the solution goes beyond their influence. Instead of commiserating or thinking, "I can't stand it when..." try thinking, "Things would be a lot better if..." That's a positive approach.

In addition, you can try to focus on the positive things about your co-workers. When you're having a problem with a particular co-worker, don't subject yourself to undue stress day after day by gritting your teeth and putting up with it. Talk with this person directly. Give him or her a chance to help improve the relationship. When you go behind a co-worker's back with gossip, bad-mouthing and backbiting, you make matters worse. You are also likely to get a reputation for being a drag on your work group and the organization. When you confront people directly, do so in a positive manner, not with a chip on your shoulder that immediately puts them on the defensive. Try to let them know that, even though you don't like their behavior, you don't lack respect for them as people. Start out by stating your positive intention about having a good relationship and then tell them directly and calmly about the behavior that's interfering. For instance, you might say, "I really respect you and I want a good relationship with you. When you [say or do]____, I get really frustrated and angry. I thought you might not be aware that you're doing this or that it affects me like it does. In the future, I would really appreciate it if you would_____[name the behavior you prefer] instead."

Confront a Co-Worker for the Sake of a Better Relationship

Is there someone in your work group who's a thorn in your side? If this person often does things that irritate you, you're likely to become negative about them—with a negative effect on your work. Be an optimist and try to make things better with this person. Plan the language you'll use in a caring confrontation. Start with this:

*_____, I really respect your abilities.
(PERSON'S NAME), I would like a better relationship with you. When you (say or do) _____,
I   feel
_____.
I would really appreciate it if you would
_____
_____*

MAKE YOUR POSITIVE ATTITUDE CONTAGIOUS

• Take action or initiative instead of feeling like a victim when your attitude is negative because of a problem with one or more of your co-workers. Don't give up before you've tried to make things better.

• Keep tabs on your negative feelings. If you start feeling negative, ask yourself what else, besides your job, might be influencing your feelings at the moment. If you think about it, you're likely to come up with another reason for temporarily feeling down. Perhaps you're just hungry. Try taking a break to get a snack. Perhaps you're fatigued, or you've been working on a particular project for too long. Turn your attention to something else for 10 or 20 minutes. Take a break and go outside for fresh air. Or, if possible, find a place to do some physical exercises.

• Think about whether you have a personal problem that's bothering you. Sometimes it's hard not to bring personal problems with you to work. But you can rarely do anything about them while you're at

work. So, decide to set them aside until a time when you can do something about them.
- Generate energy. Keep a smile on your face and in your heart during your interactions. If you can manage to show positive behavior toward others, they will respond in kind. In turn, their positive regard will help you to feel genuinely better. Research has shown that even when you feel bad, putting a heartfelt smile on your face can make you, yourself, feel better.

Remember that anything that interferes with your positive attitude is bound to affect your work, your relationships with co-workers, and your service to your customers.

Very often, you'll be pleasantly surprised when you confront a co-worker in this way. Some people are actually grateful when someone points out behavior that is interfering with the good of the group in a constructive way, so that they can do something about it. If your words and manner are calm and specific, many people perceive you as honest and caring. You might even find yourself reaping the benefits of a better relationship with his personal overall.

ACKNOWLEDGE YOUR CO-WORKERS AS INDIVIDUAL PEOPLE:
- Remember your commitment to a positive attitude and smile! Appear approachable.
- Maintain eye contact. People who don't look directly at others while talking to them tend to arouse suspicion. By paying close attention, you show your interest in what your co-workers have to say.
- Take an interest in other people's opinions, beliefs and interests. You don't have to accept them as your own, but there's a lot to be learned by finding out what other people think and care about.
- Express your curiosity about the ways in which your co-workers are different form you. Don't just talk to those who are like you. You have the power to build bridges that make your whole team more effective and the individuals within it grateful to you for including them in your circle of conversation and care.
- Be direct. Instead of talking behind your co-workers' backs, express your feelings and concerns directly.

Being positive doesn't mean being blindly optimistic. If there is a workplace where things go well 100 percent of the time, it's been a well-kept secret. But it is possible to find some good even in a bad situation. Make it your job to find the positive side of things and spread positive feelings around whenever you can. Because people spend so much time at their jobs, positive people are needed to make work upbeat and fun!

PRINCIPLE #3: ACKNOWLEDGE YOUR CO-WORKERS

Too often in a work setting, people don't talk to each other unless they want something. Whether that makes for an efficient work setting isn't clear. Sometimes an organization promotes this kind of attitude by discouraging chitchat and personal conversations.

Even in a setting like that, it's possible—and necessary—to promote goodwill among your colleagues. A warm smile, a friendly greeting, and a sincere interest in others are never out of place. When you're friendly, you help your co-workers feel appreciated and recognized as individuals rather than merely as employees. Others are more likely to help you or ask for your help when they think that you are friendly and that you recognize them as people. That makes for a cooperative work setting—one in which people work together toward common goals. Also, when you make an effort to connect to your co-workers, even briefly, you help them and yourself to overcome feelings of anonymity. You contribute to the feeling that a team is producing the work you're all doing, not people acting in isolation.

Giving Constructive Negative Feedback

Sometimes feedback is meant to give praise or thanks. But sometimes, when a co-worker's behavior is bothersome to you, the time comes to present feedback of another nature—constructive negative feedback.

Instructions: *Following the approaches to resolving problems with coworkers presented earlier, prepare to confront a co-worker whose behavior has bothered you. Use the planning form below to think out what you want to say to this person,*
either face-to-face or in writing:

<u>When you [FILL IN THE BEHAVIOUR], I felt annoyed because</u>
_____

<u>From now on, I would really appreciate it if you would</u>
_____

PRINCIPLE #4: LISTEN

Pay genuine attention to what people are saying to you. Listen to their words and the feelings being expressed **behind** those words. When someone complains, speaks up, or confronts you, pay attention to what they are saying and don't react defensively. Show genuine interest by your expressions and responses. Good listening shows support for people and lets them know you care about them and what they have to say.

If you are a direct caregiver, you know that good listening skills are crucial with patients and their families. Good listening gives you important information about what the speaker feels, needs and wants. At the same time, when you listen, your customers perceive you as caring about them. The same benefits apply in your relationships with your co-workers. Try to show the same degree of attentiveness with your co-workers that you would with patients and your other customers.

People will occasionally come to you to complain about another coworker or about the organization. You can listen and show interest in the person talking to you without becoming involved in the conflict. Negative feelings can be contagious. Don't let yourself feel defeated or defensive. Maintain your objectivity, and offer positive advice if you can. For instance, suggest that your co-worker talk directly with the person he or she is complaining about. If you can't offer positive advice, just listening to the complaint will show that you care.

Inviting Feedback from Others

Instructions: Tell your co-workers that you would welcome feedback from them. Make it easy for them to clear the air with you if you sense there's something on their minds about your behavior or attitudes.
List some of the behaviors your co-workers would like you to change:
1._____
2._____
List some other behaviors you might change to make it easier for co-workers to get along with you:
1. _____

_____

2. _____
   _____

Co-workers may sometimes engage you in conversations that are not relevant to your work and that might even threaten to interfere with your work. Know when to bow out of a conversation, firmly and with an apology. For example, you might say, "I'm sorry, but I really must get back to my desk. If I don't finish my report before lunch, I'll miss my deadline." Or, "I hate to miss out on this great conversation, but I have patients waiting." People usually understand when you speak up, and if they respect you, they won't mind continuing the conversation at a better time.

PRINCIPLE #5: APPRECIATE OTHERS

Be generous with thanks. No one person alone could possibly do all the work of a health care team. Every person on your team is a link in the chain. When just one link is missing or weak, the entire chain is broken. Every person does his or her assigned work, but only when all the people on the team work together does the entire job get done. We're all interdependent. That's what teamwork is all about.

To play a powerful role in fostering teamwork, it's important to keep in mind that, just as you need support and recognition from your supervisor and co-workers, your co-workers need the same consideration from you. When another person helps you, either because they offered or because you asked, don't take that help for granted. Express your appreciation, and make it clear that you're grateful for their assistance. A simple "Thank you for your help on this project" can be sufficient, as long as it's genuine. A statement of praise and acknowledgment of your co-worker's expertise or a job well done also shows appreciation. For example, saying, "You know, I'm really impressed with your understanding of the word processing system. I've learned a lot from working with you." Or, "Thanks for helping out with my patient. It's a big help to me when so many people need help at once." Or, "Thanks so much for covering the phones for me while I handled that difficult call. It required my full concentration, which I couldn't have given if you hadn't taken over with the other callers."

While verbal thanks are great, consider also an occasional thank you note.

Written thanks allow the receiver to savor it and even keep it. Many people even post their thank-yous, because these mean a lot and come few and far between. Thank you notes are especially appropriate when someone has gone out of the way to be helpful. Here's an example:

A Special Thank-You

Dear Saundra,
Thank you for helping me to photocopy those records. I doubt that I could have finished on time without your help. I was under a lot of pressure, and I really appreciate your pitching in.
I look forward to returning the favor!
Sincerely,
Janet

Here's a format that makes it easier to write a quick thank you note. Keep it on hand along with some small thank you note blanks, so you can jot down a quick thanks easily.

FORMAT FOR A QUICK THANKS
Dear _____
I really appreciate the fact that
_____.
It was a big help to me because
_____.
Thanks!
Sincerely,

_____

Nothing increases the likelihood that co-workers will help you out in the future as much as you thanking them for the help they gave you in the past. Just as your supervisor manages the work of your work group, it's up to you to manage your segment of the work and your interactions with the people you work with. When you need and request help from a co-worker, you are delegating your work, much the same as your supervisor delegates work to all the people on your team. If there have been times when your supervisor did not seem to appreciate you were doing, you know how it feels not to be recognized. Just as you appreciate the recognition of your supervisor and co-workers when you do something well or go out of your way to help, your co-workers value your appreciation when they help you out or do something note-worthy. If you fail to show appreciation when it's due, your co-workers may come to resent you. They'll regard you as one who makes demands, takes advantage, and doesn't appreciate their efforts. The result can be uncomfortable friction and a team that no longer runs smoothly.

Co-Workers Need Feedback, Too

A written note of appreciation thanks a co-worker for his or her help and expresses your appreciation in a way that is somewhat more formal and lasting than a spoken word of thanks.
Following the positive feedback model presented earlier, give or send a co-worker an "appreciation telegram" like the example below.

Dear Carol,
When you offered to help me prepare Ms. Schilling's end-of-month report yesterday, I felt grateful because I was feeling overwhelmed by the pressure of all the work that was involved.
Thanks a lot,
Jim

Instructions: Now, use the space below to write your own thank you note to someone who has helped you recently.

Dear_____,
_____
_____
_____
_____
Thanks
_____

Don't take your co-workers for granted. Remember the person behind the position and be generous with thanks.

PRINCIPLE #6: PITCH IN AND HELP OUT

In virtually every work setting, the object is to provide a product or service to a customer, whether this customer is someone purchasing your product service (an external customer) or someone (an internal customer) whom you help so that they can provide a product or service to external customers. You help someone to get something done, help someone to obtain a desirable product or service, or help someone to make his or her life better in some way. In health care, the focus is on helping people. How can the public expect us to help them when they need us when we fail to help each other in the course of our work? Helpfulness begins at home or, in this case, at work.

Look for ways to help your co-workers to do their jobs. Step in when you notice that someone needs help, even when it's "not your job." Offer to:

- Take a package to the mailroom if you're headed in that direction.
- Answer a telephone line for the person at the next desk so they can meet with a supervisor.
- Find a blanket for a patient waiting in a wheelchair for an X-ray because you happened to be walking by and no one else was there to help.
- Connect a physician to the right person to provide needed information.

It's no secret that health care settings are pressure cookers, even more so lately. Due to rapid change, insecure and inadequate funding, increasingly demanding patients, competition, shrinking resources under managed care, and the like, there may be fewer people to do more and more things. If you feel pressure in your job, you know you're not alone. Your co-workers are experiencing pressure, too. That's one good reason we all must do our part to help out, not only to make the workplace a better, more cooperative setting, but, on a practical level, to get done all that needs to be done. When you help out, it enhances your reputation as a team player. You set an example, and others become more willing to help you out in return. Helpfulness is contagious. And it's the friendly way to work.

PRINCIPLE #7: LIVE UP TO YOUR END OF THE JOB

When you were hired, you were selected from a pool of job applicants because it was determined that you were likely to be the best person for your particular job. Presumably, the same is true of all the people you work with. Your employers have certain expectations of you and so do your co-workers. Basically, everyone expects you to do your job to the best of your ability.

Don't let these people down. Keep your end of the bargain by doing what you've promised to do. Follow through, meet your deadlines, keep your promises. People depend on you. When you fail to complete an assignment, or to do your work on time or at a high standard, you're letting everyone down—including yourself. Your reputation is at stake, as an employee and as a team worker. You must earn your co-workers' trust and confidence.

DOES THIS SOUND FAMILIAR

Sue does a great job. Jim does a shoddy job. You can count on Sue to do things thoroughly. She responds quickly to requests and calls. She follows through. You can relax once you hear her say, "Don't worry. It's as good as done!"

Jim doesn't seem to care all that much about the quality or quantity of his work. He makes mistakes, overlooks important things, and others have to pick up after him. His supervisor and co-workers realize this.
What happens when there's more work to be done? They give it to Sue. They know they can count on Sue.
What happens? While Sue gets more and more work, but no more money for her great job performance, Jim gets less and less work. He continues to goof off and he keeps getting paid for it. Sue feels especially valued for a while and good about herself. She knows that people trust her with hard work and that she's making an extraordinary contribution. But, in the long run, she becomes resentful. Working harder and harder because people rely on her, she's carrying more than her share of the workload and getting nothing more for it. Her resentment colors her attitudes toward work. Maybe she becomes cynical. Maybe she just decides to jump shit-finding another place where a team shares the work.

When you were a new employee, it didn't take long for people to figure out what they could expect from you. If your work didn't measure up, or if you showed yourself to be unreliable, people quickly understood that they couldn't trust you to do your part. Even if you have gotten off on the wrong foot for some reason, it's not too late to do things differently. Show that you're trying. Make a real effort. When you let your co-workers down by not doing the best possible job, or by not living up to your promises, they come to resent you and to feel that you're taking advantage of them. They will come to treat you accordingly. If you earn your co-workers' trust and respect as a reliable, dependable team member, you are much more likely to develop harmonious working relationships and even some valued friendships if you want them.

To do this, it's important that you know your own limitations and what you can expect from yourself. For example, if you say, "Sure, I can have it for you tomorrow morning," when you know that you probably can't, you will approach the work with a negative attitude, knowing that you're going to fail no matter how hard you try.

Be sure to set realistic expectations of yourself before you make promises that you can't keep. Co-workers learn quickly when you let them down time after time, and their regard for you sinks. For example, it would be much better to say that you could accomplish a task by Tuesday afternoon and have it done on Tuesday morning than to set unrealistic expectations by offering to have it done on Monday but not finish it until Tuesday.

Follow through on your commitments. You'll earn people's trust.

PRINCIPLE #8: RESPECT PEOPLE'S TIME AND PRIORITIES

Pay attention to your work, and help others pay attention to theirs. Everyone who works in health care today is working under pressure. You can be pretty well assured that your co-workers feel similar pressures and stress, and that they want to pay attention to their work to get it done right.

Respect your co-workers' need for concentration, and be careful not to distract them needlessly. When your co-worker is deeply involved in a project or task and you need to ask a question, ask whether this is a good time to interrupt. Or if you need help or information urgently in order to do your job, be courteous, apologize for the interruption, and keep it brief. For example, say, "Excuse me, Kelly. I know you're really busy right now, but I need your help with something." This approach is better than barging in and making your co-worker lose her concentration.

You've probably had an experience like the one described below. How did you feel in that situation?

The Cost of Interruptions

Deborah, a social worker, sat at her desk, concentrating on a patient's chart as she constructed her part of the patient's discharge plan. Fred barged into her office, flopped down in a chair, and sat expectantly waiting for Deborah's undivided attention. Fred didn't say anything at first, but Deborah was so distracted by his presence that she lost her entire train of thought. As it turned out, Fred's reason for barging in was something that could have waited until lunch break, and Deborah, her work disrupted and her time even more pressured, felt very annoyed.

As mentioned earlier, people have different styles of working. Some prefer to concentrate hard on one particular task for a long period of time until it's either finished or at least under control. Deborah is one of those people. When her concentration is broken, she has to start her project all over again. That's not necessarily a bad way of working; it's just one style.

Other people work in short bursts. They tackle a task for a while, take a break, work a bit more, take another break, and so on. That's also not a bad way of working; it's just a different style.

Just as there are those who like to tackle one task at a time, there are others who like to work on several projects at a time, switching from one to another, but always managing to get all of them done on time. Again, not a bad way of working—just another style. Very often, when you work around the same people for a time, you get to know their individual styles of working. If you aren't already aware of how your co-workers like to pace their work, try to become sensitive to their styles, even talk to them about the subject. Know your own preferred style; become aware of how you prefer to work and how you work best. Think about whether you try to impose your style on others. With greater sensitivity, you might know that, for instance, Tom is a person you can walk right up to and interrupt and he won't mind, but Sharon will give you a really annoyed look if you say something while she's filling out paperwork.

Never sneak up on a person who is concentrating on something. Instead, announce yourself. For example, say, "Excuse me. I don't mean to interrupt, but I really need to ask you for those lab results. When you have a moment, I'd really appreciate seeing them." Or you might say, "I know you're involved in something now. Would you please let me know when you have a minute so we can discuss this patient's bill."

Be considerate of people's time. If you initiated a conversation that started out as a request for help but turned into a personal conversation, be alert to signs that your co-worker is anxious to get back to work and end the conversation. And don't take his or her signs of impatience as a personal rejection or insult.

Similarly, when a co-worker engages you in a conversation that you feel is going on too long and you would like to return to your work, find a tactful way to end the conversation without hurting the other person's feelings or giving the impression that you're uninterested or cold. For example, say, "I'd love to hear more about your vacation, Karen, but I'm really pressed for time. Maybe we can talk more over lunch." Or, "Thanks a lot for getting those forms for me. I've got to get back to my desk right now, though, or I'll get even farther behind. Let's talk again another time." If you do this well, you're likely to earn your co-worker's respect for taking your work seriously, being responsible and dependable, and handling a somewhat sticky situation with tact and respect. In fact, it's a good example to set for everyone on your team.

PRINCIPLE #9: ADMIT YOUR MISTAKES

You probably know why they put erasers on the ends of pencils. It's just a practical matter—people do make mistakes. If you're honest with yourself, you know you make them, too. Most of the time we'd like to forget our mistakes. More often than not, though, when we've made a mistake that comes to someone else's attention, the best policy is to admit it, apologize, and try to correct it. Though people are often annoyed or worse when you make a mistake that affects their work, they are usually quite understanding and even forgiving when you admit it rather than trying to cover up or make excuses.

Work in a health care environment really is interdependent, and often several people at once contribute to a particular task or service. If one person makes a mistake, it can affect the outcome of the work and possibly everyone who worked on that service. It may not always be immediately obvious where the error originated.

For this reason, when the person responsible does not own up to it, a solution to the problem may be hard to come by. In admitting a mistake or something you overlooked or neglected to do, you may not only be saving the project, you may also help your co-workers to understand what went wrong so that they can help fix it and move on to other things. Knowing that we don't create problems intentionally, co-workers appreciate it when someone takes responsibility for his or her role in problems. It takes courage to do this. You don't really need to humiliate yourself in the process by proclaiming your stupidity or getting embarrassed and feeling foolish. Just a few simple words of acknowledgment and apology and, if possible, a brief suggestion for straightening out the problem will do. Then all you can do is hope for the best.

SIMPLE APOLOGIES THAT TEND TO EARN YOU QUICK FORGIVENESS AND EVEN RESPECT

- "I must have misfiled it. I'm really sorry. I'll go look for it"
- "Frankly, I completely forgot that I promised to stop in to check on our patient. I'm sorry. I'll stop in now and explain that it was I, not you, who didn't follow through.
- "I see I listed the same item twice. I'll correct it right away."
- "I'm sorry. I didn't realize that test result was missing. I'll try to locate it right away."

Of course, there are different degrees of mistakes. Some have more serious consequences and are more difficult to fix than others. If your work is ordinarily very reliable, mistakes will be forgiven and forgotten. Meanwhile, you have set a good example by taking responsibility for your own behavior.

PRINCIPLE #10: INVEST IN OTHER PARTS OF YOUR LIFE

Too many people "put all their eggs in one basket" by relying on their jobs to provide their entire sense of identity, their self-esteem, their interests in life, their fulfillment, and even their social life. When things aren't going well at work, such people feel betrayed and disillusioned. All too often, they focus on work problems to the exclusion of everything else in their lives. When work is the only focus in a person's life, a conflict with a co-worker can cause so much stress that health problems can result and work can be adversely affected.

Such reactions can be extremely damaging, not only to a person's peace of mind, but also to a person's ability to perform well on the job and interact effectively with co-workers.

That's why we include this tip in the 10 principles. By developing other parts of your life—hobbies, community activities, family relationships, fitness, friends, involvement in the world around you—you strengthen your identity as an individual and expand your life in ways that enhance your personality and skills. You are better able to build your self-confidence, increase your concentration at work, and foster positive working relationships. You are better able to keep things in perspective. When your job fails to provide satisfaction from time to time, you know that there are other sources of satisfaction in your life that you can rely on.

Stress is so much a part of working in health care today that it can cause physical wear and tear as well as mental anguish. Become sensitive to your own unique reactions to stress and be aware of what it takes to make you feel relaxed, self-assured and in control.

ASK YOURSELF ABOUT THE BALANCE IN YOUR LIFE
- **Do you need to get more exercise, since exercise has been shown to combat stress and depression?**
- **Do you need to put more time and energy into developing your social relationships outside of work?**
- **Do you need to spend more free time doing outside activities so that job-related concerns are a smaller part of our life and your identity?**
- **Will you gain more perspective on your work by getting away from it more effectively, by taking courses, by building other skills, by taking mental vacations with are, music, dance, books, or travel?**

A lot of people can't talk about anything but their work. These people are generally regarded as narrow and boring. If this rings true for you, consider further developing your other interests through reading, traveling or hobbies. Others at work will become interested in what you have to say about your outside interests, if you want to talk about them. Or, you can keep your other interests separate if you use them as a respite from the pressures and substance of your work. Think about enrolling in educational programs, either for personal interest or for career enhancement. Everything you do and everything you learn ultimately builds your identity as a person and contributes to your personality and your ability to do a good job.

It's easy to think your current job will stay as it is forever, for better or for worse, and to assume it will always be the center of your life. But let's be frank. Today's health care environment does not encourage job stability and security for health care workers. Today you may be intensely involved with co-workers in your work group. You know that tomorrow a co-worker might leave, you might get a new supervisor, or your organization might change your job. When you have invested too much of yourself in your work, such changes have the power to make you feel as though the rug has been pulled out from under you. But, if you have more balance in your life, with your work being only one important part of it, you will be far better equipped to handle the stress of change.

When you find yourself or a co-worker becoming too involved in work and perhaps a bit obsessive about personalities or job-related problems, you (or your co-worker) need to act on this principle. Though everyone expects you to take your work seriously, it interferes with your work relationships and effectiveness when your involvement becomes so deep that it borders on obsession. Take time to ask yourself, "Why does this co-worker's behavior bother me so much? Why is it so important to me?" You'll probably find that the remedy to over-involvement is to step back a little and focus on other areas of your life. Eventually, the crisis will pass, and you'll be apt to feel a lot better about your work, your co-workers and yourself.

TAKING A LOOK AT YOURSELF

It's important for you to know how you measure up according to the 10 principles of positive co-worker relationships, so that you can identify your strengths and the areas you need to improve.

Instructions: Consider the degree to which each of the 10 principles is true of you. Place a check mark (V) in the column that best describes how you rate yourself on each principle.

	Rarely	Sometimes	Often	Almost Always
1. I respect people's differences.				
2. I think positively.				
3. I acknowledge my co-workers.				
4. I listen.				
5. I appreciate others.				
6. I pitch in and help out.				
7. I live up to my end of the job.				
8. I respect people's time and priorities.				
9. I admit my mistakes.				
10. I invest in other areas of my life.				

Identify your two main strengths from the 10 principles:
1. _____
2. _____

Identify your two main weaknesses from the 10 principles:
1. _____
2. _____

Jot down some notes on what you can do about these weaknesses.

_____
_____
_____
_____
_____

FINDING OUT HOW OTHERS SEE YOU

To gain perspective about yourself and your relationships, select a few co-workers or internal customers in other work teams and ask them to complete this short survey about your behavior from their points of view.

Dear_____ ,

I want an excellent working relationship with you. To that end, I'm asking you for feedback. How often do you
see me reflect each of the characteristics described below? Please fill out this form and give me your responses.
I'll use the results to identify ways I can make improvements that will help our relationship. Thank you!

Instructions: Consider the degree to which each of the 10 characteristics is true of me. Place a check mark () in the column that best describes how you rate me on each.

	Rarely	Sometimes	Often	Almost Always
1. I respect people's differences.				
2. I think positively.				
3. I acknowledge my co-workers.				
4. I listen.				
5. I appreciate others.				
6. I pitch in and help out.				
7. I live up to my end of the job.				
8. I respect people's time and priorities.				
9. I admit my mistakes.				
10. I invest in other areas of my life.				

What do you think are my two main strengths:
1._____
2._____

What do you think are my two main weaknesses
1._____
2._____

What's one thing that I could do to have a healthier relationship with you at work?
_____
_____

GOOD COMMUNICATION: THE KEY TO GOOD RELATIONSHIPS

The key to effective, mutually gratifying human relationships is communication—not only what people say to each other, but how they say it. In your co-worker relationships, as in your social relationships, you want to strive to treat people with dignity, courtesy and respect. After all, isn't that how you want them to treat you?

As a health care professional, you know how important it is to treat patients, their loved ones, and visitors this way. Your co-workers are no less deserving of these considerations. Just because you see them day in and day out is no reason to take them for granted or to treat them as though they don't deserve consideration.

GROUP SELF-ASSESSMENT
Instructions: Try this at a staff meeting. **First, have every person in the group write down the three principles of positive co-worker relationships that they think are followed most consistently in the group.**
Then, have every person write down the three principles that they think are not being followed consistently—with negative consequences for the group's effectiveness and morale. **Finally, on a chalkboard or a large piece of paper, tally the results.**
Celebrate the group's strengths and all the positive things you have going for you as a group. Talk about the positive things people do for each other and for the organization, and share your feelings about how you feel about each other in positive ways.
Discuss as a group one behavior on everyone's part that would, if practiced consistently, improve teamwork and harmony within the group.

Communication is as much a matter of what isn't said as it is of what is said. If you fail to say thank you when someone does you a favor, you're communicating that his or her actions don't mean very much to you. If you fail to respond when somebody talks to you, you're suggesting that he or she is not very important. If you're not clear when you give someone directions, you make it difficult for him or her to do the task adequately because you didn't say exactly what you needed or expected.

Most people interpret your failure to respond or to show appropriate interest or appreciation as indifference and snobbery. Eventually, people will respond to you in like manner, deciding consciously or unconsciously that they don't like or trust you. Clear and open communication, along with attentive responsiveness, leads to trust and cooperation. The result of good communication is that people will enjoy working with you and will be happy to cooperate and to seek your participation.

If you find that people are responding to you with indifference, take some time to examine your own style of communicating. If you find yourself in an interaction that makes you feel uncomfortable, wait until you are alone and review the situation with a critical eye toward what you may have done to make it awkward. Resolve to do things differently next time. Even people who you think absolutely hate you can become very forgiving and supportive when you show your intention and sincere effort to make things better.

DEVELOP THE DOS AND DON'TS FOR YOUR WORK TEAM

Instructions: At a staff meeting or workshop intended to strengthen teamwork, go through this plan with your co-workers. It helps you to achieve a common understanding of the behaviors that help your working relationships and gives everyone on the team a chance to commit to being a positive contributor to group morale.

1. In pairs, ask these questions of one another:
a. In what ways are you easy to get along with on the job?
b. What's one way you drive your co-workers crazy?
c. What's one way your co-workers drive you crazy?
d. What's one thing you could do to improve your relationships with your co-workers?

2. Ask people to reflect back on what they said or heard and to brainstorm as a group the "dos and

don'ts" regarding co-worker relationships in your team.

Take notes on a large piece of paper.

DO	DON'T
_____	_____
_____	_____
_____	_____
_____	_____
_____	_____
_____	_____
_____	_____
_____	_____
_____	_____
_____	_____

3. **Ask everyone to choose (and vote on) the three things on each side of the chart that are most important to the quality and harmony of the team's relationship. Narrow the list down to a small number on each side.**

4. **Finally, go around and invite each group member to commit to doing more often one or two "dos" that might help improve the quality of the team's work life.**

All that you learn about yourself and others while developing co-worker relationships will become part of your understanding of how to get along with people. Human interaction, after all, is a lifelong learning process. Understanding yourself and your own reactions to people is the best place to start.

USING THE 10 PRINCIPLES WITH DIFFICULT CO-WORKERS

Are you thinking, "This isn't hard when you're dealing with a reasonable person. But with Bob and with Helen, there's no such thing as reasonable!" Living the 10 principles described above will certainly help you with most relationships, but you may need some special tools with especially difficult people. Your differences needn't interfere with your work or keep you on edge endlessly with irritation, anger and resentment.

Let's use the case of a hypothetical co-worker, Gretchen, to illustrate methods you can use to avoid or lessen conflict with a co-worker.

If you find Gretchen merely irritating and unpleasant to work with, you might try one of these three approaches:
- **Pay attention to what makes you happy.** Instead of concentrating on Gretchen and all the ways she irritates you, take a good look at what you do like about your job: the satisfaction you get from doing your work well, the friends you have made, the little things you do during the day that bring you pleasure. Let Gretchen, for the most part, go her own way, taking up less of your mental and emotional space.
- **Enlist her help.** Gretchen may be a born complainer. One of the things that annoys you most may be that she's always complaining about how things are run and, in particular, about how you do your work. Listen to her. Or better still, ask her for constructive suggestions. She may have some very valid ideas, and when you thank her for them, she'll probably be flattered and may be easier to work with.
- **Pay her a compliment.** Everyone appreciates a compliment, and Gretchen is probably no different in that respect. Look hard to identify something you appreciate about Gretchen and tell her. Tell her what a great job she's done on something, but make sure she deserves the praise. Otherwise, you'll come across as insincere.

If you're having a more serious problem with Gretchen, do what you can by yourself to right the situation. As soon as you know there's a problem, try the following:
- **Talk it out.** Before resorting to other coping methods, try to talk with Gretchen to see whether you can come to some better resolution of the problem. You can't be sure that it will not work until you have tried talking the problem out. Say, "Gretchen, I want a better relationship with you, so I'd like to share a concern I have with you."
- **Try a win-win approach.** In situations where direct confrontation doesn't seem appropriate, approach Gretchen and ask for her advice on how the two of you could work better together. For instance, you could say, "Gretchen, I think we've had a pretty good relationship until now. But lately, I've been feeling that we're working against each other in ways that don't help either of us. Do you have any thoughts about how we could be more supportive to each other?"
- **Pick your battles carefully.** Many things about Gretchen may irritate you. It helps to identify those that are the most important

irritations before you act. If you take on every irritation, you'll drive yourself and Gretchen crazy. Before you enter into battle with anyone, figure out whether it's really worthwhile. Focus your efforts on what matters most.

- **Invest in other relationships.** Some people spend every lunchtime and every break with the same group. When a relationship within the group sours, and it doesn't seem fixable or worth fixing, the individuals involved are either stuck in an uncomfortable situation or they're left alone. By making sure that you have more than one group or person to relax with, you will give yourself alternatives that can help you through if your relationship with Gretchen continues to be troubled.
- **Be careful in whom you confide.** Most people when they have a problem with work relationships want to confide in someone about it. Surprisingly, the person you're closest to isn't always the best person to confide in. Your friend might sympathize so much with your feelings that he or she eggs you on in your fury, unable to provide a perspective that will lead to positive resolution of the problem. In other words, your friend may be so close to you that he or she can't really provide suggestions for solving the problem which would benefit you and Gretchen. If you look around, you might find someone who has some distance from the problem and might see both sides in a way that would help you.
- **Be alert for danger signs.** Every so often, stop and ask yourself, "How is my relationship with Gretchen going? What's good about it? What isn't so good, and could be improved?" If you review all your relationships periodically, you will be able to pay better attention to problems and what you can do to help them.
- **Rise above "an-eye-for-an-eye" thinking.** When co-workers come into conflict with each other, there's a natural tendency to want to get back at the other person, to take revenge. When you use this approach, you pay the price by compromising your dignity. It doesn't do anyone any good for you to engage in pettiness. You're an adult. You're a professional, and, even though you may have been hurt, there are more constructive ways to deal with a co-worker like Gretchen than to return the hurt with another one. Whether your relationship with Gretchen can be healed or not, if you stay on the high road, you'll maintain your self-respect and integrity.

Perhaps Gretchen's behavior goes beyond causing mild irritation and creating conflict. If her actions and attitudes disturb you to the point that you can't do your work effectively, or if she does something concrete to interfere with the work you're doing, it's time to take more drastic measures:

- **Invite her to lunch.** Get the problem out into the open. Tell Gretchen about the problems you're having with her. This kind of communication, perhaps in a setting that is away from the job, can be just what's needed to open the lines of communication and can go far toward healing a wounded relationship.
- **Take it to the top.** If all else fails, don't resort to bad-mouthing Gretchen to your co-workers. Let's say you've tried everything you could to ease the tension between the two of you, and still her behavior is interfering with your ability to do your work. It may be time to go to "the court of last resort"—your supervisor. It's an obvious route to take, but too often people do this too soon, before they've talked directly with the person whose behavior is troubling them. Also, they might go about doing it in a destructive way. If you talk with your supervisor about a problem with a co-worker, first, be descriptive. Don't rant and rave, and be careful to leave personalities out of it. Second, do your homework. Be prepared to describe actual incidents in which Gretchen's behavior interfered with your ability to do your job or to serve your customers. Perhaps there was a day when Gretchen misfiled charts, resulting in your spending the entire afternoon looking for what you needed. Maybe she's been lax about giving you your telephone messages, causing delays in getting information you need or in responding to the needs of others. State at the outset that you have a problem, and, in confidence, ask your supervisor's help in solving it. Tell him or her what you've already done to try to remedy the situation and that you're willing to do anything in your power to keep things running smoothly. Your supervisor will probably acknowledge that you are a valued employee and will recognize the importance of high morale and teamwork within your work group. Finally, he or she may need to intervene to rectify the situation.

IMPROVING A PROBLEM RELATIONSHIP (A THREE-WEEK EXPERIMENT)

Instructions: Take a look at yourself in a problem relationship with a co-worker. You can start making your relationships work better by identifying the principles that you have not applied effectively to this relationship.

Think of one co-worker you're having a problem with, and picture his or her face. Be conscious of how this person makes you feel—about

yourself, about your work team, and about your job. Now think about your own behavior with this person. Look over the 10 principles and select the three that, if you practiced them more consistently, might change the dynamics of this relationship for the better. Write down these three principles:

1. _____
2. _____
3. _____

Develop a plan for applying these three principles to your relationship with this co-worker for three
weeks. Remember, this is only an experiment. To make it work you must be methodical and consistent
in applying the principles you selected. In three weeks' time, see whether you have single-handedly strengthened your relationship with this person.

Write down your starting date here:_____
Write down your re-evaluation date, three weeks from the starting date:

On a 3-by-5-inch index card, write down the three principles you've selected. Keep that car in a prominent place where you can refer to it from time to time to remind yourself to carry out your plan.

Remember, your troubled relationship is very likely as uncomfortable for your co-worker as it is for you. By carrying out this experiment, you may very well create a better work environment for both of you.

CO-WORKERS LIKE IT WHEN YOU:
- Identify yourself and your department when making or answering a call.
- Take the time to transfer a call.
- Take the time and trouble to look up a telephone number.
- Ask permission when you put them on hold.
- Check back with them while they're on hold.
- Apologize for keeping them waiting.
- Take extra time and effort to track down information.
- Say please and thank you.
- Say goodbye instead of just hanging up.

- Speak calmly and distinctly, and try not to sound hurried or annoyed.

CO-WORKERS DON'T LIKE IT WHEN YOU:
- Fail to identify yourself.
- Mumble your name so they can't understand it.
- Call them honey, dear or sweetie.
- Refuse to take a message.
- Come across as short or abrupt.
- Forget to redirect their calls when they've reached the wrong department.
- Place them on hold before they've had a chance to say anything.
- Chew gum or food in their ears.
- Pick up the phone while you're still talking to someone else around you.
- Hang up without saying anything when you realize they've reached a wrong number.
- Leave them on hold indefinitely without checking back with them.
- Slam the telephone on the desk when you should have put them on hold.

RELATIONSHIPS

Employees, like customers, appreciate courtesy and consideration in telephone interactions. The guidelines that apply when dealing with the public apply equally to telephone etiquette with your co-workers who are, after all, your internal customers. Here are a few tips to remember.

HARMONY AT WORK IS WITHIN YOUR POWER

Congenial mutually helpful relationships among co-workers are essential to the smooth operation of your organization and to the quality of life you experience during the many hours you spend working. If the people you work with challenge your patience or jangle your nerves, it's up to you to take action. You can take the initiative in dealing with problem working relationships in ways that keep interpersonal differences from interfering with your work. And, if you set your mind to it, you might even be able to turn problems into opportunities that make your workplace a better place for you, your co-workers, and your customers.

By giving support and cooperation, we make each other stronger. You are in a position to help and support your co-workers—to make it easier for them to do their work. You know that nobody is a whole chain! Each one is a link. Take away one link, and the chain is broken.

You know that nobody is a whole orchestra. Each one is a musician. Take away one musician, and the symphony is incomplete.

You know that nobody is a whole hospital or nursing home or medical practice. Each one is part of the staff. Take away one person, and it isn't long before the patient suffers.

To make your organization work for every patient in need, your teamwork, cooperation and harmony with your co-workers are pivotal.

Best-Selling Books by Wendy Leebov, Ed.D.

http://www.quality-patient-experience.com/wendy-leebov-books.html

Physician Entrepreneurs: The Quality Patient Experience -- Improve outcomes, boost quality scores, and increase revenue *(Book and CD-2008)* Built around the key areas in the CAHPS survey, this book and tool-packed CD offers quick and easy techniques that physicians and practice staff can use to enhance the patient experience—without sacrificing productivity.

Wendy Leebov's Essentials for Great Patient Experiences: No Nonsense Solutions with Gratifying Results *(2008)* Specific tools that enhance the patient experience and address the difficulties staff have in delivering the exemplary care they would like to provide. High-impact strategies for moving your service excellence and patient satisfaction to a new level, resulting in higher scores on HCAHPS and CG-CAHPS.

Wendy Leebov's Essentials for Great Personal Leadership: No Nonsense Solutions with Gratifying Results *(2008)* Valuable problem-solving and leadership development for health care executives, mid-level administrators, department heads, clinical leaders, and anyone who brings a passion to their work. Each chapter captures the essence of emotionally intelligent leadership and focuses on effective solutions.

Service Quality Improvement: The Customer Satisfaction Strategy for Health Care
(Leebov and Scott) A goldmine of approaches for your service excellence initiative, that helps you build a service-oriented culture and focusing all employees on service excellence and continuous service improvement.

The Indispensable Health Care Manager: Success Strategies for a Changing Environment *(Leebov and Scott - 2003 Health Care Book of the Year)* Identifies ten role shifts needed by managers who want to add significant value to their organizations and enhance their employability. Self-assessments, case situations and concrete tools that build key leadership competencies.

Also by Wendy Leebov—practical guides that help frontline employees provide the exceptional patient and family experience
- Assertiveness Skills for Professionals in Health Care
- Customer Service for Professionals in Health Care
- Telephone Skills for Professionals in Health Care
- Resolving Complaints for Professionals in Health Care
- Working Together for Professionals in Health Care

Enrich Your Tools and Confidently Guide Your Team to the Next Level
http://www.quality-patient-experience.com/wendy-leebov-books.html

Made in the USA
San Bernardino, CA
20 November 2019